# CLICK ON

## starter

## WORKBOOK

### Student's

Virginia Evans - Neil O'Sullivan

## Express Publishing

Published by Express Publishing

Liberty House, New Greenham Park, Newbury,
Berkshire RG19 6HW
Tel.: (0044) 1635 817 363
Fax: (0044) 1635 817 463
e-mail: inquiries@expresspublishing.co.uk
http: //www.expresspublishing.co.uk

First published 2002
Fourth impression 2009

Made in EU

ISBN: 978-1-84325-753-0

# Contents

## Click on Grammar

# 1

# Hello!

## Vocabulary

**1** **a)** Look at the picture and complete the sentences. Then, ask and answer, as in the example.

1 The sun is yellow.
2 The river is blue
3 The car is red
4 The swans are White
5 The tree is brown
6 The birds are Grey
7 The grass is Green
8 The butterflies are pink
9 The boot is brown
10 The bat is black

A: What colour is the sun?
B: It's yellow.

**b)** Answer the question.

What's your favourite colour?

**2** **a)** Match the numbers to the words.

seven   eighteen   eight   twenty   sixteen
fifteen   two   five   three   nine

18   7   20   8   16   5
15   2   3   9

**b)** Ask and answer, as in the example.

A: How old are you?
B: I'm **13** years old.

**3** Find the animals.

| A | M | O | U | S | E | B | H | C | D |
|---|---|---|---|---|---|---|---|---|---|
| H | F | J | I | L | H | I | O | H | V |
| E | G | M | P | G | I | N | R | O | G |
| X | S | N | A | K | E | C | S | E | F |
| W | O | P | R | L | M | D | E | B | G |
| S | X | K | R | A | B | B | I | T | O |
| T | U | T | O | S | R | Z | D | A | L |
| V | T | U | T | Y | P | Q | O | C | D |
| W | P | J | K | R | B | C | G | E | F |
| D | Y | C | H | I | M | P | F | D | I |
| O | Q | E | Z | N | A | M | Q | U | S |
| C | A | T | R | S | K | J | L | V | H |

dog

**4** **a)** Label the clothes. Use the words in the list.

• hat • coat • shirt • shoe • dress • T-shirt
• skirt • jumper

1 hat          2 Jumper

3 Shoe          4 shirt

5 .Skirt. 6 .dress.

7 .coat. 8 .t-shirt.

**b) Ask and answer, as in the example.**

A: What's this?
B: It's a **hat**.
A: What colour is it?
B: It's **grey**.

## Grammar

**5 a) Complete the questions with Who's, What's, How.**

1 .How. are you?
2 .What's. your name?
3 .How. do you spell that?
4 .What's. your phone number?
5 .Who's. she?
6 .What's. your last name?
7 .How. old are you?
8 .What's. your favourite colour?

**b) Choose from the questions in Ex. 5a to complete the dialogue below. Then, in pairs, act out similar dialogues.**

A: 1) ..............................?
B: Helen.
A: 2) ..............................?
B: Maxwell.
A: 3) ..............................?
B: M–A–X–W–E–L–L.
A: 4) ..............................?
B: 0107246757.

**6 Complete the sentences, as in the example.**

1 This is Jason and Mary. They are/'re my parents.

2 We ............ twins.

3 Happy Birthday! You ............ sixteen now!

4 This is Niki. She ............ my mum.

5 My name is Ross. I ............ five.

**7 a) Fill in a or an, as in the example.**

1 a bell    2 **an** arm    3 **a** frog

4 **an** onion    5 **an** igloo    6 **a** pineapple

7 **an** egg    8 **a** dishwasher    9 **an** umbrella

**b) Now ask and answer, as in the example.**

A: What's this?
B: It's **a bell**.

**8** Fill in *my*, *your*, *his*, *her*, as in the example.

2 This is **my** mum.

1 Her name is Emily.

3 This is my dog. **his** name is Jack.

What's this?

4 It's **my** new computer!

5 This is a picture of **my** sister.

6 What's **your** name?

Natalie.

**9** Complete the exchanges below with the correct *personal pronoun*.

A   Mary:   How are 1) **you** today, Michael?
     Michael:  2) **I** am fine, thanks.

B   Sarah:  This is my sister. 3) **She** is only five.
     Nanny:  Hi!

C   Judy:  This is Bob and Marta. 4) **they** are my friends.
     Jim:  Hi!

**10** a) Fill in *am*, *is*, *are*.

Hi! My name 1) **is** Jim Culkin. I 2) **am** eight years old and my favourite colour 3) **is** green. This is my brother Michael. He 4) **is** seven. This is his favourite yellow T-shirt. This 5) **is** Javant. He 6) **is** ten. We 7) **are** friends.

---

**b)** In pairs, ask and answer, as in the example.

- name
- brother's/sister's/friend's name
- age
- favourite colour

*A: What's your name?*
*B: My name is Tom.*

**11** Fill in *my*, *his*, *her*.

Hello! 1) ........ name is Marta. I am ten years old. This is 2) ........ pet cat. 3) ........ name is Cleo. 4) ........ coat is black and white. This is 5) ........ friend, Yoko and this is 6) ........ dog. 7) ........ name is Rusty. 8) ........ coat is brown.

Homework 16/7

# Communication

- Introductions and Greetings

**12** Choose the correct answer A, B or C to complete the five conversations.

1  How are you?
    Ⓐ I'm fine, thanks.
    B I'm ten.
    C What about you?

2  What's your last name?
    A Pete.
    B My dad's name is John.
    C Simpson.

3  How old are you?
    A She's eight.
    B You're eight.
    C I'm eight.

4  Who's this?
A  He's George.    B  This is my mum.    C  It's a rabbit.
5  Who's he?
A  They're my brother and sister.         B  He's my brother.
C  She's my mother.

## Listening

**13** Listen and write. There is one example.

### PET CONTEST

| | |
|---|---|
| **Full Name** | Susan 1) *Whitehead* |
| **Age** | 2) ............. |
| **Address** | 14, 3) ............. Street |
| **Phone number** | 4) ............. |
| **Pet** | 5) ............. |
| **Colour** | 6) ............. |

T-shirt

## Reading

**14** Read the text. For questions 1-8, mark the correct answer A, B or C.

Home - Microsoft Internet Explorer

File  Edit  View  Go  Favorites  Help

Back  Forward  Stop  Refresh  Home  Search  Favorites  History  Channels  Fullscreen  Mail  Print  Edit

Address

Welcome to my Home Page

Hello! My name is Petra. I'm 11 years old. My mother and father are Noni and John. My brother is Michael and he is three years old. His favourite colour is green. Rachel is my sister and she is 18 years old. Snowy is Rachel's pet cat. She is white and she's 10 years old. Sniffy is my pet dog. She is black and white. She is one year old. My favourite colour is purple.

That's all about me and my family. What about you? Thanks for visiting.

Petra

Internet zone

1  Petra is ten years old.
A  Right    (B) Wrong    C  Doesn't say
2  Noni is Petra's mother.
A  Right    B  Wrong    C  Doesn't say
3  Michael is Petra's father.
A  Right    B  Wrong    C  Doesn't say
4  Sniffy is a cat.
A  Right    B  Wrong    C  Doesn't say
5  Petra's dog is one year old.
A  Right    B  Wrong    C  Doesn't say
6  Michael's pet is a parrot.
A  Right    B  Wrong    C  Doesn't say
7  Rachel's favourite colour is white.
A  Right    B  Wrong    C  Doesn't say
8  Petra's favourite colour is blue.
A  Right    B  Wrong    C  Doesn't say

## Speaking

**15** Information Exchange.

Student A: Turn to page  52
Student B: Turn to page  58

## Writing

**16** Complete this postcard. Write ONE word for each space 1-5.

Dear Mum and Dad,
   Hi! How *0) are* you? I 1) ............ fine.
   This is a picture of my friend and her dog. My friend's name 2) ............ Helen and she is 12 years 3) ............ Her favourite colour 4) ............ red. Jack is Helen's pet dog. 5) ............ is white and brown.
   Bye for now! See you soon!
Love,
Myrna

**17** Now complete the postcard to your mum and dad about your friend. Use the postcard in Ex. 16 as a model.

Dear ............,
   Hi! How ........................?
I ........................ fine.
   This is ........................ and ........................ . My friend's name ........................ and
........................ .
favourite colour ........................ .
.................... pet ............
.................... old. ................!
   See you soon!
Love,
...............

PICTURE OF YOUR FRIEND

# 2

# I'm from ...

## Vocabulary

**1** Circle the odd one out.

1 cinema, café, tree, supermarket
2 America, Turkey, Canadian, Italy
3 beautiful, fantastic, lovely, dirty
4 British, Portugal, Spanish, Chinese
5 hotel, post office, nurse, castle
6 France, Prague, Britain, Greece

**2** Fill in the gaps with the numbers or the words.

1 ...... forty-seven
2 29 ..................
3 ...... sixty-nine
4 54 ..................
5 99 ..................
6 100 ..................

**3** Use the words in the list to label the pictures. Then, ask and answer, as in the example.

• doctor • receptionist • vet • teacher

Mary
teacher

John
..................

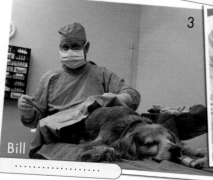
Bill
..................

Paul
..................

1 A: Who's she?
B: She's Mary.

A: What's her job?
B: She's a teacher.

**4** a) Write the names of the countries.

a zaBril ..................
b nSiap ..................
c owraNy ..................
d ehzCc epbuclRi ..................

b) Now match them to the people in the pictures. Then, act out exchanges, as in the example.

1 d
Ambroz

2
Raphael

3
Kirsten

4
Arabela

1 A: Where's Ambroz from?
B: He's from the Czech Republic.

8

**5** Fill in the opposites, then make sentences using the adjectives.

1  new ≠ o _ _
2  dirty ≠ c _ _ _ _ _
3  quiet ≠ n _ _ _ _
4  old ≠ m _ _ _ _ _

*The house is new.*

**6** Put a tick (✔) or a cross (✗) in the boxes. Then correct the false sentences.

1  This is a block of flats. ✔

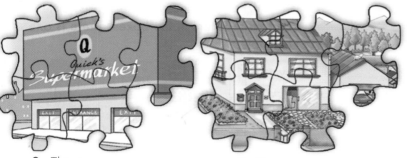

2  This is a supermarket. ☐

3  This is a cinema. ☐

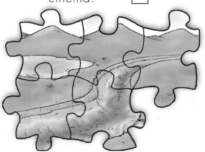

4  This is a statue. ☐

5  This is a river. ☐

6  This a park. ☐

7  This is a tree. ☐

# Grammar

**7** Complete, as in the example.

A: Are they palaces?
B: No, they aren't. They are houses.

A: ............... a postman?
B: ............... ......... pilot.

A: ............ balls?
B: ..................... ..................... ......... balloons.

A: ......... a beach?
B: ..................... .......... bridge.

A: ............... a canal?
B: ............... ............... river.

**8** Put the words in the correct order to make sentences, as in the example.

1  you/hairdresser/are/a?
   *Are you a hairdresser?*
2  from/he/not/Canada/is
   ........................................
3  is/she/nationality/what?
   ........................................
4  job/what/your/is?
   ........................................
5  city/it/fantastic/is/a
   ........................................
6  where/from/you/are?
   ........................................

9

## 9 Complete the exchanges, as in the example.

1 A: Is there a school in your street?
  B: Yes, there is.
2 A: ........... there any nice cafés in the park?
  B: No, ............................................... .
3 A: ........... there a boat on the river?
  B: No, ............................................... .
4 A: ........... there a big arch in Barcelona?
  B: Yes, ............................................... .
5 A: ........... there a bank in your street?
  B: No, ............................................... .
6 A: ........... there any trees on the beach?
  B: No, ............................................... .

## 10 Match the questions (1-8) to the answers (a-h).

| 1 | e | Is she Brazilian? | a | Yes, it is. |
| 2 | | Are there any dogs in the house? | b | No, he's from France. |
| 3 | | Is the city noisy? | c | No, they aren't. |
| 4 | | Are you my friend? | d | Yes, there is. |
| 5 | | Is Peter from Italy? | e | No, she's Spanish. |
| 6 | | Are they nine years old? | f | No, he isn't. |
| 7 | | Is there a tree in your garden? | g | Yes, there are. |
| 8 | | Is he a policeman? | h | Yes, I am. |

## 11 Write, as in the example.

She's a girl. | They are girls.

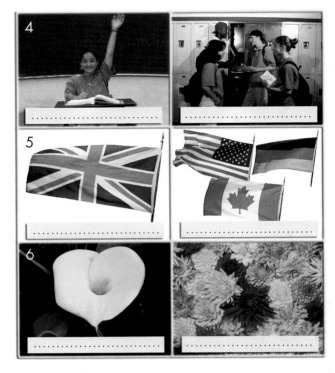

## Listening

## 12 What are these people's jobs? Listen and write letters in the boxes. There is one example.

1 Kevin C
2 Henry
3 Sally
4 Rob
5 Lou
6 Kim

## Communication

• Talking about a friend

## 13 Complete this conversation. How does Luke answer Mary? For questions 1-6, mark the correct letter A-H.

A That's Mark.      E He's twelve.
B He's from Milan.  F He's a man.
C Not bad – and you? G It's in Italy.
D Yes, he is.       H She's twelve.

M: Hello, Luke, How are you today?
L: 1) C
M: Pretty good, thank you. Luke, who's that boy over there?
L: 2) ........
M: How old is he?
L: 3) ........
M: Where is he from?
L: 4) ........
M: Where's Milan?
L: 5) ........
M: Is he Italian then?
L: 6) ........

## Speaking

**14** Information Exchange.

Student A: Turn to page 53
Student B: Turn to page 59

## Reading

**15** a) Read the article. Look at the pictures and the example. Write one word answers.

Venice is a lovely city in Italy. There are lots of beautiful

1) _____ squares, like Piazza San Marco. Venice

is famous for its old 2) ..................

and its 3) .................. with gondolas.

There are lots of 4) .................. too, but there

aren't any tall 5) .................. .

It isn't at all like busy modern cities with noisy

6) .................. . Venice is also famous

for its carnivals. It's a fantastic place to visit!

b) **What is the best title for the article?**

A  Venice, the modern city.
B  The noisy streets of Venice.
C  Venice – a great place to visit.

## Writing (a postcard from a holiday resort)

**16** a) Read the postcard and put the paragraphs in the correct order.

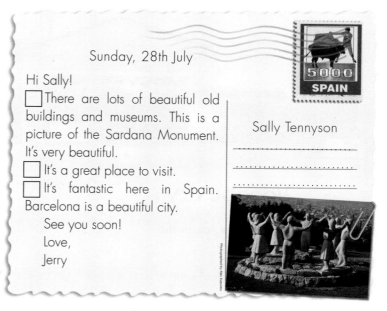

Sunday, 28th July

Hi Sally!
☐ There are lots of beautiful old buildings and museums. This is a picture of the Sardana Monument. It's very beautiful.
☐ It's a great place to visit.
☐ It's fantastic here in Spain. Barcelona is a beautiful city.
   See you soon!
   Love,
   Jerry

SPAIN

Sally Tennyson

b) **Use the information below to write a postcard to your friend.**

35 p England

• Brighton, England
• small cafés
• museums
• the Royal Pavilion

# 3 Welcome to my house!

A [ ]  B [ ]  C [ ]  D [ ]  E [ ]  F [ ]

## Vocabulary

**1 a) Complete, as in the example.**

**1** h is the fifth letter of the word **armchair**

**2** d is the ........... letter of the word **bedroom**

**3** a is the ........... letter of the word **dishwasher**

**4** c is the ........... letter of the word **Fireplace**

**5** d is the ........... letter of the word **wardrobe**

**b) What are the first, second, third and last letters of your name?**

**2 a) Read the sentences and find the parts of the house.**

1 There are trees and plants here.     garden
2 People cook in this room.            k...............
3 People sleep in this room.           b...............
4 People take a bath in this room.     b...............
5 People keep their car in here.       g...............
6 People eat in this room.             d............... ...............

**b) Now match the words to the pictures.**

**c) Make sentences, as in the example.**

C  *This is a bedroom; people sleep in this room.*

**3 Look at the pictures and do the crossword.**

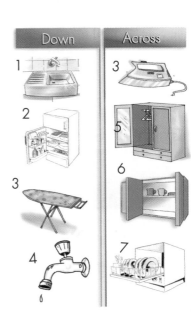

## 4 a) Read and write the name of the animal.

penguin · owl · parrot · alligator · giraffe · snake · ostrich

1 This animal is white. It's got a big body, a thick neck and sharp claws. It eats fish. ............ polar bear

2 It's got a big body and small wings. It is black and white. It can swim, but it can't fly. ............

3 It's got a small head, a long neck, and long, thin legs. ............

4 It's got a long tail and short legs, and it can swim. ............

5 It's a bird. It's got a sharp beak, and sharp claws. It can fly, but it can't run. ............

6 It's a brightly-coloured bird. It's got a long tail and wings. It can talk and fly. ............

7 It lives in the sea. It's got a big grey body. It can swim and jump. ............

8 It's a big bird. It's got feathers, a long neck and long legs. It can run, but it can't fly. ............

9 It is black and orange. It's got a big body and lives for twenty years. It can run and climb trees. ............

10 It's got a long, thin body, a small head and small eyes. It can climb trees, but it can't jump. ............

11 This animal belongs to the dog family. It is grey, brown or black and weighs about 44kg. It can run, but it can't fly. ............

wolf · tiger · dolphin · polar bear

b) Think of an animal and describe it to the class. Say what it can or can't do. The class guesses which animal it is.

## Grammar

### 5 a) Look at the table and fill in *can* or *can't*.

| | make bread | dance | paint | play tennis | play piano |
|---|---|---|---|---|---|
| Grant | ✗ | ✓ | ✓ | ✓ | ✗ |
| Nick & Sally | ✓ | ✓ | ✗ | ✗ | ✓ |
| Carol | ✓ | ✗ | ✓ | ✓ | ✗ |
| Richard | ✗ | ✓ | ✓ | ✓ | ✗ |
| Tina | ✗ | ✓ | ✓ | ✗ | ✓ |

1 Grant ........ dance, but he ........ make bread.
2 Nick and Sally ........ dance and they ........ make bread, but they ........ play tennis.
3 Carol ........ play tennis and she ........ make bread, but she ........ dance.
4 Richard ........ dance and play tennis, but he ........ make bread.
5 Tina ........ dance, but she ........ play tennis.

b) Use the prompts to ask and answer, as in the example.

1 Grant/play tennis
   A: Can Grant play tennis?
   B: Yes, he can.
2 Nick & Sally/play the piano
3 Carol/play the piano
4 Richard and Tina/paint
5 Tina/make bread

c) In pairs, ask and answer to find out what your partner can and/or can't do. Then report it to the class.

### 6 a) Underline the correct word.

Greg 1) gets/goes up early in the morning and 2) swims/walks on the beach with his dog. Afterwards, he 3) feeds/eats his dog and then he 4) has/makes breakfast on the balcony. He then 5) flies/drives to the restaurant. He 6) works/lives there as a waiter. At work Greg 7) treats/serves the customers. In the evening he 8) relaxes/talks in front of the TV or 9) thinks/reads a book. He 10) goes/grows to bed early.

**b) Describe your daily routine.**

**7**  **Complete the sentences with the verbs in brackets, as in the example.**

1  Colin works **(work)** in Prague.
2  Mum ........... **(serve)** dinner at 7:00.
3  James and Sarah ........... **(drive)** to work.
4  Maria ........... **(brush)** her hair at night.
5  The supermarket ........... **(close)** at 9:00.
6  The children ........... **(sleep)** until 10:00 in the morning.
7  The baby ........... **(cry)** when he is hungry.
8  Dad ........... **(fix)** breakfast every morning.

**8**  **a) Fill in** *at, in.*

1  Meryl sometimes works ........ the weekend.
2  The bank opens ........ 9:00 ........ the morning.
3  The trainer feeds the dolphins ........ 12 noon.
4  My grandmother sleeps a little ........ the afternoon.
5  We have supper ........ 6:30 ........ the evening.
6  Tim usually has a snack late ........ night.
7  The postman always delivers our mail ........ the morning.

**b) Make true sentences about yourself using the time phrases from Ex. 8a.**

## Communication

- **Exchanging information about abilities**

**9**  **Complete the conversations.**

1  Can you tell the time?
 A  Don't be silly.
 Ⓑ  Yes. It's half past five now.
 C  Yes. That's five thirty.

2  I can't swim, you know.
 A  Really? I can show you!
 B  Let's go and have a look.
 C  How can you?

3  Can parrots talk?
 A  Clever, isn't it?
 B  You're right!
 C  Of course they can.

4  Jake can ride his bike with no hands.
 A  How can he do that?
 B  Oh no, let's go.
 C  I'm scared.

5  Can you charm snakes?
 A  How can you do that?
 B  Don't be silly.
 C  Let's go have a look.

6  How can you do that?
 A  That's right.
 B  You're right.
 C  Oh, I don't know.

## Speaking

**10**  **Information Exchange.**

Student A: Turn to page  55
Student B: Turn to page  61

## Listening

**11**  ☉ **Listen and tick (✓) the box. There is one example.**

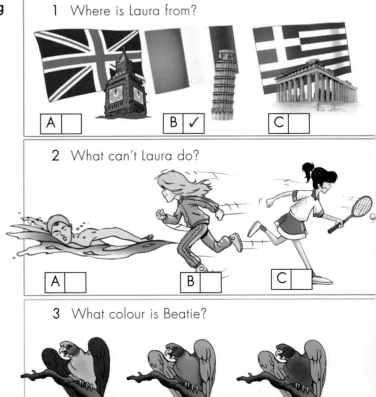

1  Where is Laura from?
2  What can't Laura do?
3  What colour is Beatie?

4  What are Laura's favourite animals?

A ☐    B ☐    C ☐

5  What is Mary's mother's job?

A ☐    B ☐    C ☐

6  What time is Laura's mother back home?

A ☐    B ☐    C ☐

# Reading

**12**  **Read the text. For questions 1-9, mark the correct answer A, B or C.**

### Penguins

There are seventeen different kinds of penguins that live in the seas and oceans around the equator and south of it. Some live near the Antarctic, others live on some islands near South America, southern Africa, Australia and New Zealand. They all belong to the bird family. They can swim very well, but they can't fly.

The Galapagos penguin lives in the waters of the Galapagos Islands near South America. It is very small. It is about 45cm tall, and weighs about 2.5kg. Its body is black and white with black wings or flippers. On its black head there is a thin white line. It runs from its throat up to the eyes. Its bill (another word for beak), is black, pink and yellow. The penguin's legs are very short.

Galapagos penguins eat small fish. They live up to twenty years. There are now only about 1,000 pairs of Galapagos penguins in the world.

1  There are twenty different kinds of penguins.
   A Right    (B) Wrong    C Doesn't say
2  They live near southern Africa.
   A Right    B Wrong    C Doesn't say

3  Penguins belong to the fish family.
   A Right    B Wrong    C Doesn't say
4  They can run.
   A Right    B Wrong    C Doesn't say
5  The Galapagos penguin lives in New Zealand.
   A Right    B Wrong    C Doesn't say
6  The Galapagos penguin isn't very tall.
   A Right    B Wrong    C Doesn't say
7  Its bill (beak) is orange, black and yellow.
   A Right    B Wrong    C Doesn't say
8  Its legs are not long.
   A Right    B Wrong    C Doesn't say
9  It lives up to thirty years.
   A Right    B Wrong    C Doesn't say

# Writing (about your daily routine)

**13**  **Choose from the verbs in the list to complete the passage about Nathan's daily routine.**

• go (x3) • be • get up • have (x2) • read
• look after • treat • watch • finish

Nathan 1) is a vet. In the morning he 2) ............ at eight o'clock. He 3) ............ to work at a quarter past nine. He 4) ............ sick animals until one o'clock. He 5) ............ lunch at half past one and then he 6) ............ back to work. He 7) ............ at six o'clock. At home he 8) ............ his dog, Bulky. In the evening, after a walk, he and Bulky 9) ............ dinner. After dinner he 10) ............ television or 11) ............ a book. At ten o'clock, he 12) ............ to bed.

**14**  **Write about your daily routine.**

I am a ............................. . In the morning I ............................. at ............................. .
I ............................. to ............................. at ............................. . I ............................. until ............................. . I ............................. lunch at ............................. and then I ............................. . In the evening, ............................. I ............................. dinner. After dinner I ............................. or ............................. At night, at ............................., ............................. to bed.

# Day in, day out

## Vocabulary

**1** Complete the days of the week. Then, answer the questions.

| April | | | | | |
|---|---|---|---|---|---|
| ................ | 7 | 14 | 21 | 28 | |
| Tuesday | 1 | 8 | 15 | 22 | 29 |
| ................ | 2 | 9 | 16 | 23 | 30 |
| Thursday | 3 | 10 | 17 | 24 | |
| ................ | 4 | 11 | 18 | 25 | |
| ................ | 5 | 12 | 19 | 26 | |
| ................ | 6 | 13 | 20 | 27 | |

- What day is the 15th of April? 6th? 26th? 7th? 30th? 11th? 17th?
- It's Tuesday. What day is it tomorrow?
- It's Sunday. What's the day after tomorrow?
- It's Friday. What day is it in three days?

**2** **a)** Do the crossword.

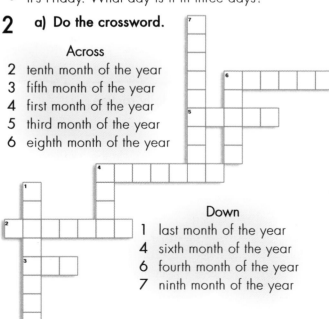

**Across**
2 tenth month of the year
3 fifth month of the year
4 first month of the year
5 third month of the year
6 eighth month of the year

**Down**
1 last month of the year
4 sixth month of the year
6 fourth month of the year
7 ninth month of the year

**b)** Which months aren't there in the crossword?

**3** Look at the noticeboard and ask and answer, as in the example.

A: When's the rock concert?
B: It's on 31st March.

**4** **a)** Write the names of the seasons.

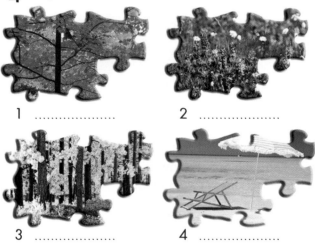

1 .................... 2 ....................

3 .................... 4 ....................

**b)** What's your favourite season?

**5** **a)** Label the pictures using the phrases in the list.

- ride a bike • go camping • take pictures
- go fishing • walk on the beach
- eat at a restaurant

1 ................ 2 ................ 3 ................

4 ................ 5 ................ 6 ................

**b)** Now use the phrases from Ex. 5a to make true sentences about you, your family, your friends, as in the example.

*I ride my bike at the weekends.*

**6**  **a)** Complete the word maps below with words from the list.

- long • slim • glasses • brown (x2) • tall
- short (x2) • curly • blue • straight • beard
- moustache • blond(e) • plump • fat
- grey (x2)

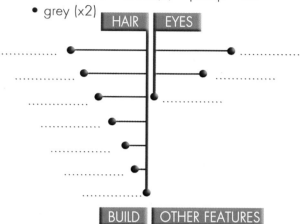

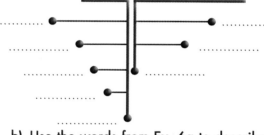

**b)** Use the words from Ex. 6a to describe the people in the pictures. Can your classmates guess who it is?

**7**  **a)** Read the description of these people's character. What is the word that describes each one? The first letter is already there.

1 Michael always tells others what to do. He's **b**ossy.
2 Jack doesn't want to work. He's **l**............ .
3 Jane always says "please" and 'thank you'. She's **p**........... .
4 Mat always tells the truth. He's very **h**........... .
5 Jeremy is quick to understand things. He's **c**........... .
6 Mary wants to help other people. She's **k**......... .
7 Chris can make people laugh. He's **f**........... .
8 George acts in an impolite way. He's **r**........... .

**b)** Make sentences about your brother/ sister; mother/father; best friend; a classmate; as in the example.

*My father is polite; he always says 'please' and 'thank you'.*

**8**  Circle the odd one out.

1 Wednesday, June , Tuesday, Friday
2 January, May, November, Winter
3 Spring, Autumn, Thursday , Summer
4 blue eyes, blonde hair, green apple , black glasses
5 straight hair , cook dinner, walk the dog, climb trees

**9**  Match the questions to the answers.

| 1 | h | What does she look like? |
| 2 | | What's he like? |
| 3 | | How often do you go to the gym? |
| 4 | | Does your mother go for walks? |
| 5 | | When is your brother's birthday? |
| 6 | | What time is it? |
| 7 | | What do you do in your free time? |
| 8 | | Where do you live? |
| 9 | | What day is it today? |
| 10 | | Do you stay up late? |

a He's kind. He always helps people.
b 10 o'clock.
c I usually play tennis.
d It's Friday.
e I live in Tokyo.
f Very often, three or four times a week.
g I never stay up late on weekdays.
h She's got short blonde hair and blue eyes.
i 1st June.
j Yes, very often.

# Grammar

**10** a) Complete the text using the correct form of the present simple of the verbs in brackets.

This is Peter. He 1) .......... (be) eleven years old. He 2) .......... (live) in London. His mother and father 3) .......... (be) from Germany so Peter 4) .......... (speak) English and German. He 5) .......... (not/ have got) a sister but he's got two brothers. He 6) .......... (want) to be a doctor like his father. Peter 7) .......... (like) all sports but his favourite sport is swimming. He 8) .......... (go) swimming every day from 7 till 9 in the evening. In his free time he 9) .......... (play) tennis and 10) .......... (meet) his friends. Peter 11) .......... (not/like) computer games but he likes to watch TV. On Sunday evenings he 12) .......... (watch) a video with his brothers or with his friends.

b) In pairs, ask and answer questions, as in the example.

A: Is Peter 11 years old?
B: Yes, he is.
A: Does he live in Paris?
B: No, he doesn't. He lives in London.

**11** What do they do in their free time? Write, as in the example.

ride (my) bike

do the shopping

2 .......... Peggy stay at home on Fridays?
No, ....................
........................
........................ .

play the flute

3 .......... you play the piano, Sarah?
No, ....................
........................
........................ .

eat out

4 .......... George and Pat cook on Friday evening?
No, ....................
........................ .

look after his brother

5 .......... Peter play with his friends on Saturday mornings?
No, ....................
........................ .

1 Does John go to the beach at weekends? No, he doesn't. He rides his bike at weekends.

**12** Look at the table. What do these people do when they are on holiday? Ask and answer, as in the example.

| always | ✓✓✓ | sometimes | ✓ |
| usually | ✓✓✓ | never | X |
| often | ✓✓ | | |

| | play golf | play tennis | go swimming | read books | watch videos |
|---|---|---|---|---|---|
| Mark | ✓✓✓ | ✓ | ✓✓ | ✓✓✓✓ | X |
| Jack & Jill | X | ✓✓ | ✓✓✓✓ | ✓ | ✓✓✓ |
| Wilfred | ✓✓ | X | ✓✓✓✓ | ✓✓✓ | ✓ |
| Tom & Mary | ✓ | ✓✓✓ | X | ✓✓ | ✓✓✓✓ |

A: Does Mark play golf when he is on holiday?
B: Yes, he usually plays golf when he is on holiday.

**13** Circle the correct word.

1 Sandra has dinner **at** / **on** 6:30.
2 Jim works a lot and he can't sleep **in** / **at** night.
3 The banks aren't open **in** / **at** the afternoon.
4 Her children don't like getting up early **in** / **at** the morning.
5 Jessy goes on holiday **in** / **on** June.
6 Claire reads books **in** / **on** the evenings.
7 Bob's birthday is **in** / **on** 13th September.
8 She has guitar lessons **at** / **on** Wednesdays.
9 We go ice-skating **in** / **on** winter.
10 They don't fly kites **in** / **at** October, do they?

# Speaking

**14** Information Exchange.

Student A: Turn to page 56
Student B: Turn to page 62

# Communication

• Making plans for the weekend

**15** Complete the conversation, then in pairs act out similar dialogues.

John: What a day, Mike!
Mike: 1) B
John: Well, it's Friday and there's a weekend ahead.
Mike: 2) .......
John: Oh, I always sleep late.
Mike: 3) .......
John: Really? Can I come with you tomorrow?
Mike: 4) .......
John: Great. We can meet around 2 pm. Is that OK?
Mike: 5) .......

A Of course you can!
B I know. Lots and lots of classes.
C Sure. It sounds fine!
D Me too. But in the afternoon I usually go and play football.
E What do you do on Saturday mornings, John?

# Listening

**16** Listen to Sarah and Joan talking about different activities. What does each person do? For questions 1-6, write a letter A-H next to each person. You will hear the conversation twice.

People

1 Joan    [D]
2 Ann     [ ]
3 David   [ ]
4 Pete    [ ]
5 Paul    [ ]
6 Sarah   [ ]

Activities

A plays football
B watches a video
C plays basketball
D has a piano lesson
E goes swimming
F goes to the theatre
G has a French lesson
H goes to the gym

# Reading

**17** Read the text. Are the sentences True *(T)* or False *(F)*?

## All about Vanessa

Vanessa Marie Atler is a gymnast. Her parents are Ted and Nanette, and her brother is Teddy. She also has a dog. His name is George. Vanessa's hobbies are movies, table tennis, and computer games. Vanessa goes to the gym every day. She usually gets up at 7:00 and has yoghurt and fruit for breakfast. Sometimes she goes for a walk before she goes to the gym. Her favourite colours are blue and green, the colours of the ocean. TV shows that she likes are *Seinfeld*, *Road Rules*, and *I Love Lucy*. Vanessa enjoys food like apple pie, salad, pasta, yoghurt, and Mexican food.
She always drinks carrot juice before each practice. Vanessa's birthday is on 17th February.

1 Vanessa's brother's name is Ted.                    F
2 She hasn't got a pet.                                ...
3 One of her hobbies is computer games.               ...
4 Vanessa always goes for walk in the morning         ...
5 She always has a drink of carrot juice
  before she practises every day.                     ...
6 Vanessa's birthday is 7th February.                 ...

# Writing (my favourite season)

**18** Complete the text with phrases from the list.

• go to the beach • playing beach-volley
• go abroad • swimming and sunbathing
• go water-skiing

I really like summer. It's sunny and it's warm. We usually 1) ..................... .......... for our holidays. We 2) ..................... every day. I like 3) ....... ............................... . I sometimes 4) ............. ..................... but I prefer 5) ..................... .....................

**19** Now write about your favourite season. What do you like to do? What do you usually/often/always/never do?

23

# 6

# How much is it?

## Vocabulary

**1** **a) Use the words in the list to label the pictures.**

- chicken • eggs • lemons • beef
- bread • oranges • milk • fish
- grapes • cheese

1 ...............
2 ...............
3 ...............
4 ...............
5 ...............
6 ...............
7 ...............
8 ...............
9 ...............
10 ...............

**b) What other kinds of fruit, vegetables, seafood can you think of?**

**2** **a) Match the sentences to the notices.**

1 You can buy fish here. ☐B
2 You can buy trousers and suits here. ☐
3 You can buy bread here. ☐
4 You can buy make-up and perfume here. ☐
5 You can buy milk and cheese here. ☐
6 You can buy hats, scarves and belts here. ☐

Department Store

A Dairy Products
B Seafood
C Meat & Poultry
D Bakery
E Beauty Products
F Accessories
G Menswear
H Sportswear

**b) What can you buy in the other two sections?**

**3** **a) Read about Shana, Martin and Louise. Who wants to buy what? Look at the pictures and write the names.**

Shana has got a pink pair of trousers and wants to buy a pink shirt to match them. She needs to buy a pair of jeans, too. She's got lots of T-shirts but she doesn't have many pairs of socks. She's got £25 to spend.

Martin wants to buy a baseball cap and a green top. He really needs a jacket because he doesn't have one. He also wants to buy a pair of woollen gloves but he's already got one pair. He's got £45 pounds to spend.

Louise needs to buy a woollen jumper and a pair of black gloves. She also wants to buy a pair of boots and a scarf. She's got £50 to spend.

£5    £15
£20    £5

1 ...................

£10
£38    £12
£35

2 ...................

24

3 .................

b) Now, act out exchanges, as in the example.

A: How much money has Shana got?
B: She's got £25.
A: What can she buy with it?
B: She can buy ... but she can't buy ... .

**4** Look at the town plan and act out exchanges, as in the example.

A: Where's the chemist's?
B: It's in Malven Road, next to the post office.

## Grammar

**5** Fill in *some* or *any*, as in the example.

1 I need some apples to make a pie.
2 Would you like .............. sugar in your tea?
3 We don't need to buy .............. bananas.
4 Can you buy .............. milk and eggs, please?
5 There isn't .............. coffee in the cupboard.
6 I'd like .............. spaghetti and meat, please.

**6** Look at the shopping list and act out exchanges, as in the example.

| | | | |
|---|---|---|---|
| tomatoes | 1 kilo | cheese | ½ kilo |
| carrots | 6 | bread | 2 loaves |
| potatoes | 1½ kilos | pasta | 1 kilo |
| lemons | 4 | Coke | 2 bottles |
| eggs | 12 | | |
| meat | 3 kilos | | |

A: How many tomatoes do we need?
B: 1 kilo.

A: How much bread do we need?
B: Two loaves.

**7** Fill in: *a pair of, some, a/an, any.*

1 There aren't ........ eggs in the fridge.
2 Tom, put on ........ clean T-shirt.
3 Would you like ........ pasta for dinner?
4 ........ apple a day keeps the doctor away.
5 Here are ........ oranges. Make the juice.
6 We need ........ socks.

**8** Match the sentences to the pictures.

• Don't touch this! • Smell the flower!
• Come to Daddy! • Click twice on the mouse! • Open wide! • Try this burger!

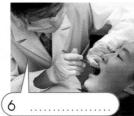

25

# Communication

• Buying food (at the greengrocer's)

**9** Circle the correct response.

1 A: Can I help you, sir?
   B: a Yes, please. How much are the carrots?
      b Right. And how many potatoes do we need?

2 A: They're 70p a kilo.
   B: a Have you got them in yellow?
      b I want two kilos, please.

3 A: Would you like some peppers? Nice green peppers they are!
   B: a Oh, I'm sorry. They're over there.
      b Oh, that's a good idea. Three peppers, please.

4 A: Anything else?
   B: a No, thank you.
      b Yes, how much do you want?

5 A: Two kilos of carrots, and three green peppers. That's £2.90, sir.
   B: a Here you are and keep the change.
      b What else can I do for you?

# Listening

**10** 🔊 Listen and fill in the order form below. There is one example.

| SMARTFAM<br>Clothes for the whole family | Order form<br>Name: Mrs L Fairchild<br>Acc/No.: 395 277 K | | | |
|---|---|---|---|---|
| Items | Department | Colour | Size | Price |
| shorts | sportswear | ........ | ........ | £7.99 |
| ........ | menswear | yellow | ........ | £20.99 |
| scarf | ladieswear | ........ | – | £5.00 |

# Speaking

**11** Information Exchange.

Student A: Turn to page 57
Student B: Turn to page 63

# Reading

**12** Read the review about Carlo's Italian restaurant. Choose the best word (A, B or C) for each space (1-9).

## Carlo's

1) ............ Italian food your favourite? Well, 2) ................ the sea, at the end of High Street, there is a fine Italian restaurant. You can park your car at the car park 3) ............ the beach or go there by bus and 4) ............ it is, at the corner of High Street and Devon Road.

Carlo's isn't 5) ............ expensive restaurant. It offers excellent pasta – Spaghetti alla Milanese, Spaghetti con Fungi (mushrooms) etc at very good prices. Try 6) ............ seafood and fish, too, a shrimp salad or any kind of pasta with shrimps.

For dessert you can 7) ................ a piece of Italian apple pie, a fresh fruit salad or 8) ............ pineapple and mango ice cream.

Carlo's Restaurant is open from 10:30 am until 11 pm 9) ............ day.

Address: Carlo's Restaurant
106 High Street
Tel: 78035120

| 1 | (A) Is | B Has | C Can |
|---|---|---|---|
| 2 | A in front of | B under | C near |
| 3 | A in | B on | C behind |
| 4 | A where | B that | C there |
| 5 | A a | B an | C – |
| 6 | A its | B his | C her |
| 7 | A have | B has | C be |
| 8 | A some | B any | C much |
| 9 | A any | B every | C some |

# Writing (a recipe)

**13 a)** Label the pictures using the verbs in the list.

    • boil • grate • slice • beat • spread • fill • mix • pour

1 ....................      2 ....................      3 ....................      4 ....................

5 ....................      6 ....................      7 ....................      8 ....................

**b)** Use four of the verbs from Ex. 13a to complete the recipe below.

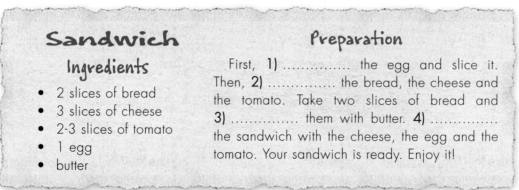

### Sandwich

**Ingredients**

- 2 slices of bread
- 3 slices of cheese
- 2-3 slices of tomato
- 1 egg
- butter

### Preparation

First, **1)** .............. the egg and slice it. Then, **2)** .............. the bread, the cheese and the tomato. Take two slices of bread and **3)** .............. them with butter. **4)** .............. the sandwich with the cheese, the egg and the tomato. Your sandwich is ready. Enjoy it!

**14 a)** What do you need to make an omelette? Tick (✓) the ingredients, then say, as in the example.

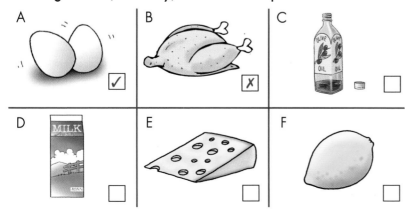

A [✓]    B [X]    C [ ]

D [ ]    E [ ]    F [ ]

*We need two eggs. We don't need any chicken.*

**b)** Use the rest of the verbs from Ex. 13a to complete the steps below, then put them in the right order.

| a |  | ........ the mixture into the pan. |
| b |  | ........ the cheese. |
| c |  | ........ the eggs. |
| d |  | ........ the eggs with cheese. |

**c)** Use your answers in Exs. 14a and b to write a recipe for an omelette. Use the recipe in Ex. 13b as a model.

## The Indefinite Article (A/An)

- We use **an** before words which begin with a **vowel** sound (a, e, i, o, u).
  *an apple*     *an orange*     *an umbrella*
- We use **a** before words which begin with a **consonant** sound (b, c, d, f, g, h, j, k, l, m, n, p, q, r, s, t, v, w, x, y, z).
  *a dress*     *a snake*     *a pet*

## The verb "to be" affirmative

| Long Form | Short Form |
|-----------|------------|
| I am | I'm |
| you are | you're |
| he is | he's |
| she is | she's |
| it is | it's |
| we are | we're |
| you are | you're |
| they are | they're |

## Personal Subject Pronouns

| Singular | Plural |
|----------|--------|
| I | we |
| you | you |
| he | |
| she } | they |
| it | |

I → always with a capital letter
you → in the singular and plural
he → for a man or a boy
she → for a woman or a girl
it → for an animal or a thing
they → for people, animals or things

### • The Indefinite Article A/An

**1** Fill in *a/an*, as in the example.

1  an apple     2  ..... clock     3  ..... orange

4  ..... boot     5  ..... iron     6  ..... rose

**2** **a) Put the words in the correct column.**

- fish • armchair • shirt • family • parrot
- elephant • tree • aeroplane • teacher
- coat

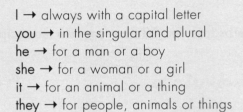

| a | an |
|---|---|
| ............... | ............... |
| ............... | ............... |
| ............... | ............... |
| ............... | |
| ............... | |
| ............... | |
| ............... | |

**b) Look around and say what there is in the classroom.**

*There is a blackboard.*

• Personal Subject Pronouns

**3** Fill in the correct *subject pronoun*, as in the example.

1  she         2  ............         3  ............

4  ............         5  ............         6  ............

**4** Complete the sentences, as in the example.

1  This is an apple.
   It's red.
2  My name is Helen.
   ............ am 16.
3  This is Will.
   ............ is my brother.
4  This is a jumper.
   ............ is orange.
5  This is Rachel, Danielle and Susan.
   ............ are my friends.
6  This is David.
   ............ is my dad.
7  This is Miranda.
   ............ is my sister.
8  This is Fluffy and Snowball.
   ............ are my pet rabbits.

**5** Fill in the questions. Then look at the pictures and act out similar exchanges.

Tom/my friend        my bicycle/new

A: ..................?   A: ..................?
B: This is Tom. He's my   B: This is my bicycle.
   friend.                   It's new.

A

my mother's umbrella/
black

B

Peter/my father

C

Eloise/my teacher

D

snake/black and white

• The verb "to be"

**6** Fill in *'m/am*, *'s/is*, *'re/are*, as in the example.

1  It 's/is a red dress.
2  She ............ Mary.
3  You ............ my friend.
4  This ............ my dog.
5  I ............ from Paris.
6  They ............ my parents.
7  He ............Patrick.
8  It ............ an orange.
9  We ............ brothers.
10  They ............ yellow cars.

**7** Use the prompts to make sentences, as in the example.

1  I/16 years old.
   I'm sixteen years old.
2  Thunder/my horse.
   ..................................
3  My brother/eight.
   ..................................
4  I/Mike's brother.
   ..................................
5  His last name/Thomson.
   ..................................
6  The mouse and the cat/grey.
   ..................................
7  My sister and my brother/18 years old.
   ..................................
8  This/my family.
   ..................................

29

## The verb "to be"

| Negative | | Interrogative | | Short Answers | |
|---|---|---|---|---|---|
| Long Form | Short Form | | | | |
| I am not | I'm not | Am | I ...? | Yes, I am. | No, I'm not. |
| you are not | you aren't | Are | you ...? | Yes, you are. | No, you aren't. |
| he is not | he isn't | | he ...? | Yes, he is. | No, he isn't. |
| she is not | she isn't | Is | she ...? | Yes, she is. | No, she isn't. |
| it is not | it isn't | | it ...? | Yes, it is. | No, it isn't. |
| we are not | we aren't | | we ...? | Yes, we are. | No, we aren't. |
| you are not | you aren't | Are | you ...? | Yes, you are. | No, you aren't. |
| they are not | they aren't | | they ...? | Yes, they are. | No, they aren't. |

- We do not repeat the whole question in short answers. We only use *Yes* or *No*, the subject pronoun and the appropriate verb form.
- We use the **long form** of the verb **to be** in **positive short answers**.
  *Is she OK? Yes, **she is**.* (NOT: ~~Yes, she's.~~)
- We use the **short form** of the verb **to be** in negative **short answers**.
  *Are you from Spain? No, **I'm not**.* (NOT: ~~No, I am not.~~)

## Plurals

Most nouns take **-s** in the plural.
*bed - bed**s***          *friend - friend**s***          *book - book**s***

## There is / There are

| | SINGULAR | PLURAL |
|---|---|---|
| Affirmative | There is **a** dog./There's **a** dog. | There are **some** dogs. |
| Negative | There isn't **a** dog. | There aren't **any** dogs. |
| Interrogative | Is there **a** dog? | Are there **any** dogs? |

- **There are** hasn't got a short form.
- We use **there is** to give a list of single items.
  ***There's*** *a dress, a coat and a hat in the room.*
  (NOT: ~~There are~~ *a dress, a coat and a hat in the room.*

| Short Answers | |
|---|---|
| Is there ...? | Yes, there is. |
| | No, there isn't. |
| Are there...? | Yes, there are. |
| | No, there aren't. |

- In short answers we use **Yes, there is/are**. or **No, there isn't/aren't**. We do not repeat the whole question.

30

• Simple Present

**1** Use the prompts to write sentences, as in the example.

1 he/go swimming/ weekend
*He goes swimming at the weekend.*

2 My friends and I/ go cycling/weekend
...........................
...........................
...........................

3 Brian/take his dog to the beach/morning
...........................
...........................
...........................

4 Martha/work in the garden/morning
...........................
...........................
...........................

5 Chris and Tom/have lunch in the park/ noon
...........................
...........................
...........................

6 Mrs Smith/look after her granddaughter/ afternoon
...........................
...........................
...........................

7 Jane/ride her horse/ every day
...........................
...........................

8 Mum/give me a bath/every day
...........................
...........................

9 Tom and Sarah/go skiing in the mountains/every year
...........................
...........................
...........................
...........................

10 Doug/play golf/ weekends
...........................
...........................
...........................
...........................

**2** Use the verbs in brackets to complete the sentences, as in the example.

1 I live (live) in Ankara.
2 She .............. (go) to bed early in the evening.
3 He .............. (eat) an apple every morning.
4 Tom and Michael .............. (ride) their bikes to school every day.
5 He's a dolphin trainer. He .............. (work) in an aquarium.
6 "Are you a policeman?"
"No. I'm a fireman. I .............. (put) out fires."
7 In the evenings, Sally .............. (help) her sister with her homework.
8 Every month Jerry .............. (send) a letter to his pen-friend.
9 Diana .............. (brush) her teeth twice a day.
10 Dan and Betty .............. (drive) to the office every day.
11 The supermarket .............. (close) at nine in the evening.
12 Ruth .............. (catch) the train to town in the mornings.

41

• Can

**3** **Complete the sentences with** *can* **and/or** *can't*.

1 I ........... make a cake, but I ........... make a pizza.
2 Juan ........... sing and he ........... dance.
3 We .......... fly to New York, but we ........... drive there.
4 John .......... read and write French.
5 I .......... say the alphabet in English, but I .......... say it in German.

6 We ........... look after your cat, but we ........... look after your snake.
7 Jim ........... drive a car, but he ........... fly a plane.
8 My baby sister .......... walk and talk.
9 Tina .......... draw, but she .......... write her name.
10 Mat .......... count and Al .......... read.

**4** **Look at the pictures. Follow the lines then use the prompts to ask and answer, as in the example.**

1 Matthew/cook spaghetti
  A: *Can Matthew cook spaghetti?*
  B: *No, he can't.*
2 George/speak English
  A: ...........................................................
  B: ...........................................................
3 Helen/play tennis
  A: ...........................................................
  B: ...........................................................
4 Jo/ride a bicycle
  A: ...........................................................
  B: ...........................................................

5 Helen/speak English
  A: ...........................................................
  B: ...........................................................
6 Matthew/play the guitar
  A: ...........................................................
  B: ...........................................................
7 Tim/play the guitar
  A: ...........................................................
  B: ...........................................................
8 George/cook spaghetti
  A: ...........................................................
  B: ...........................................................

42

## • Prepositions of Time

**5** **a) Complete the table with phrases from the list.**

- 7:00 • half past four • noon • ten o'clock
- the evening • the afternoon • night

| in | the morning, ......................................... |
|----|--------------------------------------------------|
| at | the weekend, ....................................... ........................................... |

**b) Make true sentences about yourself using the verbs below as well as the phrases from the table in Ex. 5a, as in the example.**

- wake up • climb trees • ride my bike
- go to school • have dinner • have breakfast
- look after my pet • go to bed

*I wake up at 7:00 in the morning.*

**6** **Complete the text with *in* or *at*.**

John gets up early 1) .......... the morning. After a walk and a shower, he is ready for breakfast 2) .......... 7:30. 3) .......... 8:15 he leaves home and catches the bus to the city. He's at work 4) .......... half an hour. 5) .......... noon he has lunch. He gets home 6) .......... 6:00 7) .......... the evening. John has supper 8) .......... 7:00. He doesn't work 9) .......... weekends, so he sleeps late 10) .......... the mornings on those two days.

## • Revision Section (Units 1 - 4)

**7** **Circle the correct item.**

1 Claire ................. draw, but she can't write.
  A can't    B can    C she

2 A baby ................. ride a bicycle!
  A can't    B hasn't    C isn't

3 "................. does that wolf live?"
  "In China."
  A What    B Who    C Where

4 Are ................. any peacocks in the zoo?
  A they    B there    C that

5 Look at those beautiful ............. in the garden!
  A cat    B cat's    C cats

6 ................. long does a wolf live?
  A Who    B Why    C How

7 Is he a pilot? ................. planes?
  A Can he fly  B He can't fly  C He can fly

8 ................. she got a sister?
  A Does    B Have    C Has

9 ................. jockey rides horses in races.
  A An    B A    C These

10 "What ................. his job?"
  "He's a hairdresser."
  A 'm    B 's    C 're

11 I have lunch ................. noon.
  A on    B in    C at

12 We feed our dogs ................. the afternoon.
  A at    B to    C in

13 "What time is it?" "................. half past three."
  A This is    B It's    C That is

14 "Is this ................. ruler?"
  "Yes, it's my ruler."
  A his    B her    C your

15 ................. alligator has got a long tail.
  A A    B An    C Those

16 "Where are the children?"
  "................. in the living room."
  A He's    B You're    C They're

17 This is Megan's mirror and ................. are her brushes.
  A they    B that    C these

18 Johnny and Peggy have got a boat. ............. boat is red and white.
  A Their    B They    C There

19 "Are you a nurse?"
  "No, I ................. ."
  A am    B 'm not    C aren't

20 That is my ................. friend.
  A mothers'  B mother's  C mothers

## Present Simple

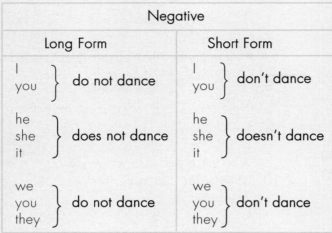

| Negative | |
|---|---|
| **Long Form** | **Short Form** |
| I<br>you } do not dance | I<br>you } don't dance |
| he<br>she } does not dance<br>it | he<br>she } doesn't dance<br>it |
| we<br>you } do not dance<br>they | we<br>you } don't dance<br>they |

| Interrogative | Short answers |
|---|---|
| Do { I<br>you } dance …? | Yes, I/you **do**.<br>No, I/you **don't**. |
| Does { he<br>she<br>it } dance …? | Yes, he/she/it **does**.<br>No, he/she/it **doesn't**. |
| Do { we<br>you<br>they } dance …? | Yes, we/you/they **do**.<br>No, we/you/they **don't**. |

- We form the third person singular in the negative with **does not/doesn't + main verb**.

- We form all the other persons in the negative with **do not/ don't + main verb**.

- We form the third person singular in the interrogative with **does + personal pronoun + main verb**.

- We form all the other persons in the interrogative with **do + personal pronoun + main verb**.

## Adverbs of Frequency

- Adverbs of frequency tell us **how often** something happens.
  These are:
  always (100%)    sometimes (25%)
  usually (75%)    never (0%)
  often (50%)

- Adverbs of frequency go **before the main verb** but **after the verb to be**:
  *She **sometimes eats** fruit.*
  *He **is usually** tired after work.*

## Prepositions of Time

We use **on** with

- days: *on Wednesday, on Fridays, on weekdays, etc*
- dates: *on 1st May, etc*

We use **in** with

- months: *in June, etc*
- seasons: *in the winter/ spring/summer/ autumn, etc*
- years: *in 2000, in 1979, etc*
- the expressions: *in the morning/afternoon/ evening*

## The Imperative

- We form the imperative with the **base form of the verb** without the subject.
  *Close the window!*

- We form the negative imperative with **do not/don't** and the base form of the verb.
  *Don't be late!*

- We use the imperative to tell someone what to do or not to do.
  *Open the door!*
  *Don't make any noise.*

- give orders: *Don't shout!*

- give instructions: *Mix the eggs with the flour first.*

- offer something: *Have some cake.*

- make a request: *Don't use your camera, please.* or *Please don't use your camera.* (To sound polite, we usually add the word **please** at the beginning or at the end of the sentence.)

### • Countable / Uncountable Nouns

**1** These are Sarah's and Pat's shopping lists. Write *C* for countables and *U* for uncountables next to each item.

| Sarah's List | | Pat's List | |
|---|---|---|---|
| sweetcorn | ..... | stamps | ..... |
| bread | ..... | hat | ..... |
| potatoes | ..... | jewellery | ..... |
| pasta | ..... | belt | |
| eggs | ..... | scarf | ..... |
| meat | ..... | perfume | ..... |
| milk | ..... | T-shirt | ..... |

**b)** Now make your own shopping list, as in the example, then tell your partner.

*I need to buy some carrots ...*

**2** Look at the picture and the prompts and say what there *is/isn't*, *are/aren't* in the picture, as in the example.

- beef • biscuits • carrots • pears • oranges
- spaghetti • peaches • grapes • shrimps
- milk • burger • pizza • lemons • apples
- cheese • strawberries • onions • cake
- eggs • pasta • ice cream • potatoes
- peppers • fruit salad • pineapple • mango
- tomatoes • fish

*There isn't any beef but there's a biscuit.*

49

## • A/An/Some/Any

**3** Underline the correct word, as in the example.

1 Is that **a/an** apple on the table?
2 Where can I buy **some/any** milk?
3 We don't need **any/a** coffee or tea.
4 Can I have **a/some** ice cream?
5 Buy **a/some** loaf of bread.
6 Can I have **any/some** soup, please?
7 Go to the chemist's! We need **some/a** medicine.
8 There aren't **any/some** mangoes left.
9 There is **some/any** chicken in the fridge.
10 Can I have **a/some** piece of apple pie?
11 I don't want **a/an** egg.

**4** Look at the picture, then act out exchanges, as in the example.

• milk • meat • carrots • tomatoes • cheese
• fish • peppers • grapes • bananas • cake
• eggs • a bottle of soda • oranges • apples
• a bottle of Coke

A: *Do we need any milk?*
B: *No, we don't. There is some in the fridge.*

## • How much/How many

**5** Fill in: *how much*, *how many*, *some*, *any*.

A: Is there **1)** any sugar left?
B: No, there isn't.
A: **2)** ................ sugar do we need?
B: A kilo.
A: Have we got **3)** ............... bread?
B: Yes, we've got a loaf and **4)** ........ bread rolls.
A: **5)** ............... tomatoes have we got?
B: Two or three, I guess. You can buy **6)** ............ .
A: I'd like to buy a pizza.
B: A pizza? **7)** ............... is it?
A: £5.50.
B: We can make it at home, can't we?
A: Yes, we can. I'd like **8)** ........... biscuits, too.
B: Well, buy them, then.
A: Have we got **9)** ........... coffee?
B: Yes, we've got **10)** ............ .
A: Anything else?
B: Buy **11)** ............... cherries but don't buy
  **12)** ............... olives, we've got a lot.

## • The Imperative

**6** Look at the pictures. Then, use verbs from the list to complete the sentences, as in the examples.

• wash • read • play • be • talk • drink
• eat • do

1 Don't be late for school!    2 Do your homework!

3 ............. comics!    4 ........... your milk!

# Information Exchange

| Animal: | giraffe |
|---|---|
| Description: | long neck, short body, long legs |
| Colour: | yellow and brown |
| Size: | 5.3m to 6m tall |
| Lives in: | East Africa, Angola, Zambia |
| Eats: | leaves |

| Animal: | PANDA |
|---|---|
| Description: | ................................................. |
| Colour: | ................................................. |
| Size: | ................................................. |
| Lives in: | ................................................. |
| Eats: | ................................................. |

**Ask questions to complete
the panda fact file.**

You need to arrange three piano lessons for the week with your music teacher. You can't miss Language, Maths or Science lessons. Look at your timetable, then ask and answer, as in the example.

Teacher: Can you have a lesson at .................... on ....................?
Student: Er ... no, I can't because it's ........................ and I can't miss it.
Teacher: What about .................... at ....................?
Student: Yes, I'm free then.

| | MONDAY | TUESDAY | WEDNESDAY | THURSDAY | FRIDAY |
|---|---|---|---|---|---|
| 8:30-9:15 | English | Spanish | History | Spanish | English |
| 9:15-10:00 | Maths | Science | Spanish | Maths | Maths |
| 10:00-10:45 | Geography | Maths | Science | English | Science |
| 10:45-11:00 | | | BREAK | | |
| 11:00-11:45 | Computers | Geography | Maths | Art | History |
| 11:45-12:30 | Computers | English | English | Art | Free |
| 12:30-13:15 | Music | Gym | Computers | Library | Science |
| 13:15-13:45 | | | LUNCH | | |
| 13:45-14:30 | English | Free | Sport | Spanish | Spanish |
| 14:30-15:15 | History | Library | Sport | Geography | Free |

**UNIT 6**

**Here's some information about a restaurant. Answer student A's questions.**

Italian?

Where?

open/Sundays?

serve/breakfast?

car/park?

**Ask student A questions to find out about**  **Restaurant.**

## KENG'S
### Chinese Restaurant

open Monday to Saturday 12:30 pm to 10:00 pm

more than 100 dishes

chicken: our speciality

big car park

opposite the bank in Greenway Street

NAME: ..................................................... DATE: .....................................

CLASS: ..................................................... MARK: .....................................

(Time: 20 minutes)

## Vocabulary & Grammar

**1 Fill in the missing words. Use only one word.**

1 "How ......... are you?" "Eleven."
2 This ......... my brother. His name is Bob.
3 Jim is my pen-......... .
4 "What's this?" "This is ......... orange."
5 "How do you ......... your name?"
  "M-A-R-Y."
6 "......... is Susan?" "She's Mary's mother."
7 "What ......... is your T-shirt?" "Blue."
8 This is Greg and Tom. ......... are my friends.
9 Toby is seven ......... old.
10 "Hello! ......... are you?" "Fine, thanks."

**2 Circle the correct item.**

1 This is my brother. ......... name is Steven.
  A My        B His        C Her

2 This is a ......... shoe.
  A red        B last        C seven

3 "How ......... your sister?" "She's fine."
  A are        B am        C is

4 This is Arthur. He's my ......... .
  A mother        B brother        C sister

5 "What's ......... name?" "My name is Sarah."
  A his        B her        C your

6 Ribbi is my pet ......... .
  A rabbit        B hat        C number

7 This is Helen. ......... is my friend.
  A He        B She        C It

8 "What is it?" "......... a dress."
  A He's        B She's        C It's

9 Stuart and I ......... friends.
  A am        B is        C are

10 "What's .........?" "It's my dog, Pluto."
  A this        B it        C he

## Communication

**3 Complete the questions.**

A: ...........................?

B: He's my father.

A: ...........................?

B: His name is Kevin.

A: ...........................?

B: He's 35.

A: ...........................?

B: She's my mother.

A: ...........................?

B: Her name is Laura.

A: ...........................?

B: She's 30.

65

NAME: ............................................. DATE: ...................................

CLASS: ............................................. MARK: ...................................

(Time: 20 minutes)

## Vocabulary & Grammar

**1 Fill in the missing words. Use only one word.**

1 There ............. a statue in my neighbourhood.
2 This is a big block of ............. .
3 There aren't ............. buildings in the park.
4 Omar is Turkish; he's from ............. .
5 He isn't Canadian; he ............. American.
6 "............. are you from?" "Poland."
7 "............. you from Spain?" "No, I'm not."
8 "What ............. is Grace?" "She's British."
9 There ............. some cafés in my town.
10 "What's ............. job?" "I'm a vet."

**2 Circle the correct item.**

1 "........... afternoon. Can I help you?"
  A Good      B Noisy      C Quiet

2 Jane .......... a doctor; she's a nurse.
  A isn't      B aren't      C am not

3 Julio's from .......... .
  A Portuguese  B Chinese  C Argentina

4 ".......... he Italian?" "No, he isn't."
  A Am      B Are      C Is

5 This river isn't clean; it's very .......... .
  A old      B modern      C dirty

6 Is there .......... park in your neighbourhood?
  A some      B a      C any

7 There are some benches in the .......... .
  A block of flats  B supermarket  C park

8 There .......... any dirty beaches in this country.
  A isn't      B are      C aren't

9 This street is very quiet; it's not .......... .
  A noisy      B tall      C lovely

10 "Is this 39 Baker Street?" "Yes, .......... is."
  A she      B he      C it

## Communication

**3 Complete the dialogue.**

A: Good morning. 1) ...................................?
B: I want to see the doctor, please.
A: Of course. 2) ...................................?
B: Smithson. Jake Smithson.
A: 3) ...................................?
B: S-M-I-T-H-S-O-N
A: 4) ...................................?
B: 38B, Bond Street.
A: Right. And 5) ...................................?
B: It's 0120623789.
A: Thank you.

67

NAME: ...................................... DATE: ......................

CLASS: ..................................... MARK: .....................

(Time: 20 minutes)

## Vocabulary & Grammar

### 1 Fill in the missing words. Use only one word.

1 Martha .............. a book in the evenings.

2 ".............. Paul ride his bike to school?" "No, he catches the bus."

3 Oh, no. It's 8:30! I'm .............. for school!

4 I go out with my friends .............. Fridays.

5 Stephen is .......... ; he can make people laugh.

6 "Do you always watch a video in the evenings?" "Yes, I .............. ."

7 "What's Ruth ..............?" "She's very kind."

8 ".............. is your birthday, Sam?" "On 11th March."

9 "What does Mike .............. like?" "He's really tall!"

10 "How .............. do you go to the gym?" "Two or three times a week."

### 2 Circle the correct item.

1 Jake's birthday is .......... March.
   A on        B in        C at

2 Mary is very honest; she always .......... the truth.
   A tells      B says      C asks

3 Jim .......... fly a kite every week.
   A don't      B isn't      C doesn't

4 These hotel rooms are very .......... .
   A perfect    B plump      C comfortable

5 Children like to make snowmen .......... winter.
   A on        B in        C at

6 Her hair is short and .......... .
   A slim       B fat        C curly

7 ".......... day is it tomorrow?" "Tuesday."
   A What       B Who       C When

8 "Do Terry and Laura go on picnics at the weekends?" "Yes, .......... ."
   A do they    B they do    C they don't

9 George .......... tells lies. He hates it.
   A always     B usually     C never

10 The Smiths like to travel .......... .
   A tour       B abroad      C holiday

## Communication

### 3 Complete the questions.

A: Dad! 1) ..............
   ..........................?
B: Yes, I'm very late for work!
A: 2) .....................
   .........................?
B: I start at 8:00.
A: Oh dear!
B: What? 3) ..............
   .................... now?
A: It's 8:00 Dad.

A: 4) .........................., Jackie?
B: My birthday's on 21st April.
   5) ..........................?
A: Mine is on 13th May.
B: Oh! That's today! Happy birthday then!
A: Thank you!

73

NAME:..................................................... DATE:..................................

CLASS:..................................................... MARK:..................................

(Time: 20 minutes)

## Vocabulary & Grammar

**1 Fill in the missing words. Use only one word.**

1 .............. many apples are there in the basket?
2 "What .............. are you?" "Small."
3 I need to buy .............. pair of jeans.
4 You can buy a doll at the .............. shop.
5 Don't buy .............. bananas; we've got a lot.
6 "I want to buy some stamps." "Go to the .............. office."
7 How .............. does this T-shirt cost?
8 ".............. 's the butcher's?" "In Apple street."
9 Is there .............. beef in the fridge?
10 I often go .............. for clothes on Saturdays.

**2 Circle the correct item.**

1 "I want to buy a dress." "Go to the .......... department."
   A menswear  B womenswear  C sportswear

2 .......... ride your bike in the street; it's dangerous.
   A Don't        B Do            C Doesn't

3 Let's go to the Body Shop; I want to buy some face .......... .
   A wash         B brush         C clean

4 "Where's the baker's?" "It's .......... the left of the chemist's."
   A at           B on            C in

5 I never wear smart clothes; I like .......... clothes.
   A casual       B fashion       C style

6 How much .......... do we need?
   A eggs         B sugar         C mushrooms

7 Go to the .......... to buy peppers.
   A baker's      B greengrocer's C newsagent's

8 Are there any .......... in the jar?
   A butter       B cheese        C olives

9 The bank is .......... the supermarket.
   A between      B opposite      C next

10 Jane wants to buy .......... new clothes.
   A some         B any            C many

## Communication

**3 Match the exchanges.**

1 [ ] Look! How about some cake?

2 [ ] Do you want the chocolate cake or the carrot cake?

3 [ ] It's only £1.20

a How much is the carrot cake?

b OK then. Let's take that.

c Mmm. That's a good idea.